A HISTORY OF THE United States of America THROUGH ART

Eleanor Van Zandt

Wayland

Titles in this series

A History of Britain through Art

A History of France through Art

A History of Italy through Art

A History of the United States of America through Art

To my mother

Cover: *Unveiling the Statue of Liberty* by Edward Moran
Title page: *The Declaration of Independence* by John Trumbull

Series Editor: Rosemary Ashley
Book Editor: Joanne Jessop
Designer: Jean Wheeler

First published in 1995 by Wayland (Publishers) Limited
61 Western Road, Hove, East Sussex, BN3 1JD, England

British Library Cataloguing in Publication Data
Zandt, Eleanor Van
History of the United States Through Art. – (History Through Art Series)
I. Title II. Series 973

ISBN 0–7502–1555–0

Typeset by Jean Wheeler
Printed and bound by
L.E.G.O. S.p.A, Vicenza, Italy

Acknowledgements
The Publishers would like to thank the following for allowing their pictures to be reproduced in this book:
AKG London 12. 37, 40; The British Museum 5; Camera Press 43; Bridgeman Art Library 7, 8, 17, 27, 34; Peter Newark's American Pictures 9, 20, 21, 23, 29, 36; Peter Newark's Military Pictures 31; Photri Inc title page, 11, 13, 15, 39; Range Pictures Ltd. cover, 19, 25, 33, 35; Visual Arts Library 45 © Robert Rauschenberg/DACS, London/VAGA, New York 1995.

CONTENTS

The First Americans 4
The Plymouth Colony 6
Settlers from Many Lands 8
Farm Life 10
'The British Are Coming!' 12
The Declaration of Independence 14
Washington's Surprise Attack 16
The 'Era of Good Feelings' 18
New Frontiers 20
The Trail of Tears 22
The Gold Rush 24
Slavery 26
The Civil War 28
The Battle of Gettysburg 30
Liberty and a New Life 32
The Railway 34
The Wild West 36
'The Yanks Are Coming' 38
The Great Depression 40
'The Marines Have Landed' 42
A World Power 44
Glossary 46
Timeline 46
Books to Read 47
Index 48

The pictures in this book span nearly four hundred years of American history – from the founding of the first European colonies to the present day. The work of the different artists in this book shows us some of the many events and experiences that have shaped the history of the United States of America.

THE FIRST AMERICANS

The first people to settle in North America travelled from Asia across a land bridge into present-day Alaska more than 25,000 years ago. When Christopher Columbus 'discovered' the American continent, he thought he had landed in the East Indies, so he called the people living there 'Indians'. However, American Indians are more accurately called Native Americans.

The Native Americans in this picture were painted by John White, one of the first English colonists and governor of a small colony founded in 1587 on Roanoke Island, near the coast of present-day North Carolina.

The Manner of Their Fishing by John White (died c 1593). You can see this painting in the British Museum, London.

A month after founding the colony, White sailed back to England for badly needed supplies. England was then at war with Spain, and no ships were available to take White back to Roanoke until 1590. When he finally returned, all the colonists had vanished. The name of a nearby Indian village – Croatoan – was found carved on to a tree. But the colonists were not at Croatoan, or anywhere else. Perhaps they were captured by Native Americans and eventually were married to them. Today, some Native Americans living in this area claim to be descended from the settlers of this 'Lost Colony'.

White made many drawings and paintings of the Native American way of life. In this painting, *The Manner of Their Fishing*, White shows some Native Americans wading in shallow water to spear fish and others in a canoe in deeper water catching fish with a net on a pole. The light cast by the fire in the canoe attracted fish to the nets at night. The reed fence across the water was also used to catch fish. Notice how White shows not only the top view of the water but also the underwater view. He wanted to include as much information as possible in his painting.

The manner of their fishing

THE PLYMOUTH COLONY

The British eventually established thirteen colonies along the east coast. The first permanent settlement was Jamestown, Virginia, founded in 1607. The second was the Plymouth Colony in Massachusetts, settled in 1620 by a group of people known as Pilgrims because of their wanderings in search of religious freedom.

The Pilgrims called themselves 'Separatists' because they had separated from the Church of England. In 1609, after a law had been passed in England forcing everyone to attend Church of England services, the Separatists went to live in Holland. But they were unhappy because their children were adopting Dutch ways and forgetting they were English.

In September 1620, the Separatists, along with some non-Separatist colonists, set sail for the 'New World'. After a voyage of sixty-five days, their little ship, the *Mayflower*, reached the north-east coast of North America. Before going ashore, the colonists all made a promise to each other to obey the laws they themselves would make in their new colony. This promise, known as the Mayflower Compact, was the first step towards self-government and democracy in the New World.

Only half the colonists survived the harsh winter of 1620. But with the help of some Native Americans they soon learned how to plant native vegetables, such as sweet corn and pumpkins. The following autumn, the Pilgrims gave a great feast to thank God for a successful harvest. They invited their Native American friends to this thanksgiving celebration. Two hundred years later, President Abraham Lincoln named the last Thursday of November a national day of Thanksgiving. Today, the main feature of Thanksgiving dinner is turkey – a bird native to North America and probably part of the first Thanksgiving meal of 1621.

Pilgrims Going to Church
by George Henry Boughton (1833–1905). This painting is part of a private collection.

The Pilgrims are walking to church through the snow. As you can see, they dressed plainly. Their church services included very long sermons. Children had to sit quietly for two or three hours, and they were tapped on the head if they fell asleep.

◀ Most of the men are carrying guns in case they come across wild animals that they can kill for food. The early colonists had to rely on hunting for their meat supplies.

SETTLERS FROM MANY LANDS

Many European nations founded colonies in North America. The French settled in what is now Canada and in Louisiana; the Dutch in New Amsterdam, which later became New York. The Swedes, who introduced the log cabin to North America, settled in Delaware. Many German people came to Pennsylvania in search of religious freedom. The Spanish founded settlements in Florida and, on the other side of the continent, in the present-day states of Texas, New Mexico and California.

In 1681, William Penn founded Pennsylvania, which means 'Penn's Woods'. As a young man, Penn joined the Society of Friends, or Quakers, and was sent to prison many times because of his religious beliefs. He wanted to start a colony where people of different religions could all worship God as they pleased. When the king of England, Charles II, who owed a favour to Penn's family, gave Penn some land in North America, he established his colony.

The painting on page 8 shows Penn (with outstretched arm) making a treaty with some Native Americans. Penn always respected the Native Americans' claims to the land, and they, in turn, never attacked his colony. Penn promised freedom of religion and a say in the government to all those who came to Pennsylvania. Among the early settlers were the Mennonites, members of a strict Protestant sect from Germany. Their well-kept farms and simple way of life can still be seen in Pennsylvania today.

◀ ***Penn's Treaty with the Indians, November 1683*** by Benjamin West (1738–1820), This painting is part of a private collection.

West studied art in Philadelphia before going to Europe. After studying in Italy he settled in London, where he became a very successful artist and president of the Royal Academy.

The picture below shows the mission church in the Spanish settlement of Santa Clara de Asis in California, founded in 1777. As early as the 1500s, the Spanish were building churches to convert the Indians to Christianity. Notice the horses and cattle, which the Spanish had introduced into the New World. The horse changed the way of life for many Native American tribes. The Plains Indians, for example, became superb horsemen, riding hundreds of kilometres to hunt buffalo.

Santa Clara de Asis by an unknown artist.

This picture shows the settlement of Santa Clara de Asis, in California, as it would have looked in the 1780s.

FARM LIFE

The vast areas of fertile land in North America attracted many settlers, who created thriving farms out of the wilderness.

In the south there were large farms, called plantations, where most of the work was done by slaves. Many of the plantations were located on rivers and could be reached by ships, so they could trade directly with Britain. Tobacco, rice and indigo were grown on plantations and sent to Europe in exchange for manufactured goods. But many basic goods were made on the plantation, which might have a blacksmith, a shoemaker, a cooper (who made barrels) and a weaver to weave cloth. There might also have been a kiln for making bricks and a mill for grinding flour.

Farther north, farms were smaller and worked by their owners and sometimes a few servants. The Pennsylvania farm in this painting was owned by David Twining, the foster father of the artist – Edward Hicks. Mr Twining stands in the foreground holding a bucket, while Mrs Twining sits nearby reading from a book (probably the Bible) to a little boy. Hicks has painted himself as the little boy. The Black farmhands would have been freemen, not slaves; Mr and Mrs Twining were Quakers, and they would not have owned slaves.

Hicks painted this picture in the 1840s from memory, showing the farm as it looked in 1787. He was one of the best of the folk, or 'naive', artists, who had little or no formal training. There were no art schools in the colonies, and few painters had opportunities to travel to Europe to receive formal art training. But people wanted paintings, of themselves and their homes and farms, so untrained painters supplied them. Their work does not have the

▲ Turkeys were raised as food by Native Americans as early as AD 1000, and the colonists soon adopted this custom. Benjamin Franklin proposed that the turkey be chosen as the national bird, but Congress voted by a small margin in favour of the bald eagle.

technical skill of a trained artist. Compare this painting, for example, with the one by Benjamin West on page 8, with its well-balanced composition and life-like figures. However, many folk artists, including Hicks, had a keen eye for detail, and their paintings have a lively quality. They are a valuable record of everyday life in the days before the invention of photography.

The Residence of David Twining, 1787 by Edward Hicks (1780–1849). This painting is in the Abby Aldrich Rockefeller Folk Art Collection, Williamsburg, Virginia.

Hicks was a Quaker preacher and one of the most famous folk artists.

'THE BRITISH ARE COMING!'

For a hundred years, the Thirteen Colonies handled their own affairs with little interference from Britain. But when the British Parliament began to impose taxes that the colonists felt were unfair, there was strong protest. In 1775, this protest led to the War of Independence.

The colonists resented British taxes because they had no say in the matter; they were not represented in the British Parliament. Groups calling themselves the Sons of Liberty held noisy meetings to demand independence. Resistance was especially strong in Massachusetts.

In 1773, several men dumped crates of tea from a British ship into the Boston harbour as a protest against the tax on tea. In response to the 'Boston Tea Party', the British passed what the colonists called the 'Intolerable Acts'. These laws closed the port of Boston, dissolved the Massachusetts assembly (government) and sent in British troops. The Sons of Liberty began forming a volunteer militia known as the 'minutemen' because they were prepared to fight 'at a minute's notice'.

Boston Tea Party

A coloured lithograph by Currier and Ives dated 1846. Currier and Ives was a firm that specialized in scenes of American everyday life and historical events .

The colonists dressed up as Indians, boarded a British ship and threw a cargo of tea overboard. They were protesting against the British tax on imported tea.

Paul Revere, a Boston silversmith, was one of the leading Sons of Liberty. On the night of 18 April 1775, he learned that the British were about to march on Concord, 32 km away, to destroy the supply of arms there. He quickly saddled his horse and rode off, stopping at every town and village on the way to Concord to warn people that the British were coming. The British set out for Concord the next morning. When they reached Lexington, a town near Concord, they found a line of armed minutemen on the green. The British commanding officer ordered them to disperse, but they resisted. Shots were fired, and eight minutemen were killed. At Concord, larger numbers were waiting. They drove the British back, at a cost of seventy British and forty-nine American lives. The War of Independence had begun.

Midnight Ride of Paul Revere by Grant Wood (1892–1942). This painting is in the Metropolitan Museum of Art, New York.

Grant Wood painted portraits and scenes from history and everyday American life in a hard, plain style. This painting of Paul Revere's famous ride has a mysterious, eerie quality. The village and surrounding countryside are unnaturally tidy and the powerful light casts dramatic shadows, which make us feel the excitement of the event.

THE DECLARATION OF INDEPENDENCE

The First Continental Congress met in Philadelphia in 1774. Delegates came from most of the Thirteen Colonies to protest against the Intolerable Acts. At that time few of them were demanding independence. They considered themselves loyal subjects of King George III.

The delegates resolved to stop trading with Britain as long as the Intolerable Acts were in force. When war broke out in 1775, the Congress met again. They raised an army and appointed George Washington as commander-in-chief. In a last effort to achieve a peaceful settlement, Congress sent a petition to the king. He refused to read it.

On 11 June 1776, Congress voted in favour of breaking their ties with Britain and chose a committee to write the Declaration of Independence. Most of this inspiring and moving document was written by Thomas Jefferson, who later became the nation's third President.

The Declaration states: 'We hold these truths to be self-evident, that all men are created equal, that they are endowed by their Creator with certain unalienable Rights, that among these are Life, Liberty and the pursuit of Happiness.' It goes on to say that governments are created by people to protect these rights, and that if a government actually destroys them, people have a right to 'throw off' that government. In the eighteenth century this was a shocking thing to say.

The signing of the Declaration took place on 4 July. This detail from a painting of the event shows Thomas Jefferson presenting the Declaration to John Hancock (in the chair), who was president of the Congress. To Jefferson's left is Benjamin Franklin, whose wise words guided the Congress through many sticky moments, and other members of the committee, including John Adams (with hand on hip), who became the second President.

The Declaration of Independence by John Trumbull (1756–1843). This is in the Yale University Art Gallery.

Trumbull fought on the American side in the War of Independence.

WASHINGTON'S SURPRISE ATTACK

Although the American army was up against the best-trained army in the world, they had certain advantages. They were fighting on – and for – their own land, and they were skilled in surprise attacks from hidden positions. Above all, the Americans had General George Washington. He had a cool head, courage, determination and the ability to command loyalty.

In December 1776, the war was not going very well for the Americans. They had been pushed out of New York City by the British. Washington had moved his army to the west bank of the Delaware River to protect Philadelphia. The British were clustered around New York and New Jersey, to the east. They had stopped fighting for the winter, as was the custom in those days. Washington was desperate. Half of his army would be discharged at the end of the year, to be replaced by raw recruits – or no one – and the enemy would then have an easy march to Philadelphia. So he planned a surprise for them.

On Christmas Eve, Washington and 2,400 men crossed the icy river in a fleet of small boats during a snow storm. The next morning they advanced on Trenton, where the British forces were asleep after their Christmas festivities. A few cannon shots down the main street persuaded the stunned soldiers to surrender. The Americans took 900 prisoners and 1,200 weapons. Only two lives were lost.

The Trenton victory was a great boost for American morale. Men hurried to join the army, and Congress gave General Washington more support. Then in 1778, France, Britain's traditional enemy, signed a treaty with the Americans. Together they fought until the war was finally won, at Yorktown, Virginia, on 19 October 1781.

Washington Crossing the Delaware
by Emanuel G. Leutze (1816–68). This painting is in the Metropolitan Museum of Art, New York.

This picture is somewhat misleading since the American 'Stars and Stripes' flag was not used until 1777. In 1776, Washington would have flown the Grand Union flag, which had the British Union Jack in place of the stars. The thirteen stripes on the American flag represented the Thirteen Colonies. After independence the Union Jack was replaced with the stars. A star was added for every state that joined the union. Today there are fifty stars on the American flag.

THE 'ERA OF GOOD FEELINGS'

When this picture was painted, in 1819, Philadelphia was still the Union's largest city, with 130,000 people. As the cradle of American liberty, it celebrated the Fourth of July – Independence Day – in style. These citizens, dressed in their best clothes, are clearly bursting with national pride and good spirits. This was the beginning of the 'era of good feelings', which spanned the years 1818 to 1825. It was a time of growth and prosperity as more states joined the Union.

Before the era of good feelings, however, there had been a period of conflict. Between 1812 and 1814, the USA had again been at war with Britain. The British had captured the new capital city, Washington, and burned down the White House, the Capitol and several other government buildings. The Americans won the war, but it had created tensions within the country. The north-eastern states had strongly opposed the war and even threatened to leave the Union. Some states refused to contribute money and men for the war effort.

There was also disagreement within the country over the division of power between the national, or federal, government and the governments of the different states. The Federalists favoured a strong central government, and the Democratic-Republicans wanted more power to be held by the states.

By the time President James Monroe was elected, the disagreement had quietened down. Monroe enjoyed the support of most Americans. He also established friendly relations with Britain, and both countries agreed to cut down on their numbers of weapons. The border between the USA and Canada was drawn as far west as the Oregon Territory. With peace at home and abroad, the nation had cause to celebrate.

Fourth of July, Center Square, Philadelphia
by John L. Krimmel (1789–1821). This painting belongs to the Historical Society of Pennsylvania in Philadelphia.

◀ This young boy contributes to the celebrations by dancing to the music of a fiddler. By the time of independence there were about 40,000 free Black Americans. Many of them fought on the colonists' side in the War of Independence.

NEW FRONTIERS

In 1775, a year before the Declaration of Independence, an explorer named Daniel Boone cleared a trail over the Appalachian Mountains into Kentucky. Thousands of hunters, trappers and settlers made their way over this 'Wilderness Road' in search of a better life. The great American move west was under way.

Those pioneers who travelled westwards faced great hardships and dangers, including possible attacks from Indians whose way of life was being threatened. But clearly the prize seemed worth the risks: by 1790 over 100,000 people had crossed the Appalachian Mountains into what was then called the Northwest Territory.

In 1803, President Thomas Jefferson made what is probably the best property deal of all time. France had recently regained the Louisiana Territory from Spain. This huge area reached from the present state of Louisiana all the way up the Mississippi River to Canada and as far west as

On the Oregon Trail
by Albert Bierstadt (1830–1902). This painting is in the National Cowboy Hall of Fame, Oklahoma City.

In this painting, a group of pioneers are heading west in a covered wagon, along with their horses, cattle and other farm animals. The magnificent landscape inspired many painters. Albert Bierstadt was born in Germany and emigrated to the USA with his family in 1832. He specialized in western landscapes.

the Rocky Mountains. If France were to colonize this region it would block any further American expansion to the west. Jefferson asked his ambassador in Paris to try to buy New Orleans, the port on the Mississippi, near the Gulf of Mexico, so that American trade down the Mississippi could continue. To the ambassador's surprise, the French government offered to sell all of Louisiana Territory for only $15 million. The USA acquired another 2,144,500 sq km of land, doubling its area.

The following year, Jefferson appointed two army officers, named Meriwether Lewis and William Clark, to make an expedition across the continent. Lewis and Clark spent two years travelling from St. Louis, on the Mississippi, to the west coast. They mapped the river routes, made notes of the plants and animals in the region and made friendly contact with some Indian tribes. They had opened a path through the Louisiana Territory into Oregon, via the Oregon Trail, which pioneers soon began to follow in their push westwards.

Sacagawea Guides Lewis and Clark during the Expedition of Exploration 1804-06
This is a lithograph taken from a painting by Alfred Russell.

Sacagawea, a young Indian woman from the Shoshoni tribe, was guide and translator for Lewis and Clark and their team of explorers. She led them through the Rocky Mountains to the shores of the Pacific Ocean.

THE TRAIL OF TEARS

Not all the people who moved west did so of their own free will. Many Native Americans were forced to give up their land to make way for European settlers. This painting shows the forced removal of the Cherokees from their homeland – one of the saddest stories in Native American history.

The Cherokees originally lived mainly in northern Georgia and Tennessee. They were farmers, who had adopted many of the white people's ways. In 1791, the federal government had made a treaty with the Cherokee nation, giving them independence. By the early 1800s many Cherokees had become Christians, and a Cherokee named Sequoya had invented a way of writing the Cherokee language. The Cherokee nation had a newspaper, *The Cherokee Phoenix*, and their own elected government.

Over the years the state of Georgia took away pieces of Cherokee land. When gold was discovered there in 1828, Georgia passed a law requiring the Cherokees to leave. The Cherokee nation appealed to the Supreme Court to uphold their rights, and the Court did so. But President Andrew Jackson, who had bitter memories of Indian attacks on his town during the War of Independence, sided with the state of Georgia.

In 1838, the army moved the Cherokees off their land. Their destination was the Indian Territory in what is now the state of Oklahoma, a distance of some 970 km. This forced journey westwards was called the Trail of Tears because of the hardships suffered along the way. It was wintertime, and many died, from starvation, disease and the cold. Out of 17,000, only 13,000 completed the journey. Today there are about 50,000 Cherokees in the USA. About 45,000 live in Oklahoma; some 5,000 live near their original homeland, on a reservation in North Carolina.

The Trail of Tears ▶
by Robert Lindneux (1871–1970)

This painting shows the Cherokees making their way west under a stormy sky, escorted by soldiers.

At the centre of this painting, a little girl holds her mother's hand and clutches a puppy, which is too young to walk all the way and has to be carried. The mother dog looks up anxiously at its puppy. The girl's mother is carrying a baby on her back in the traditional Indian way; the baby would have been securely strapped on to a board beneath the shawl. Notice that many Cherokees are riding in covered wagons like those used by European pioneers. (See the painting on page 20.)

THE GOLD RUSH

There have been many gold rushes in history, but the most famous was the California Gold Rush of 1849. Eighty thousand people raced to the west coast in a bid to make a fortune.

The first nuggets of gold were found on 24 January 1848 by James Marshall, a workman at Sutter's Sawmill, in present-day Sacramento. The mine's owner, John Sutter, tried to keep the discovery secret; he was hoping to buy the land. But California itself was about to change hands; the USA had gained the territory from Mexico in the recent Mexican War (1846–48). So Sutter could not yet buy the land.

For a while Sutter managed to keep his secret. California was thousands of kilometres away from the east; there was no coast-to-coast railway and no telephone. Although the telegraph had recently been invented, a wire network across the USA had not yet been created. Gradually, though, the news of the gold discovery leaked out. It was confirmed by President James Polk in his farewell address in December 1848. Now the race was on. People from all over the world quit their jobs, mortgaged their houses and farms, deserted their families and struck out for the California gold fields.

When they got to California, the Forty-Niners, as they were called, lived in rough mining camps and shanty towns. Men spent their days crouched in stream beds, sifting gravel in the search for gold, and their nights drinking and gambling. For a real spree they went to San Francisco. In1848, San Francisco was a small village; however, by the end of 1849 it had a population of 25,000 and a reputation for wild living.

▲ The young man is probably telling his sweetheart that once he makes his fortune they can get married.

New York Post Office: Reading News of the Gold Rush by William Mount (1807–1868). This painting is in the Suffolk Museum at Stony Brook, Long Island.

The dreams of instant wealth can be seen on the faces of these people as they gather in a New York City post office to read the latest news from the gold fields. The posters on the wall advertise sea passage to the west coast. In those days there was no Panama Canal, so ships had to sail around Cape Horn, at the southern tip of South America. Thousands took this trip in the hope of finding their fortunes in the California gold fields.

SLAVERY

Slavery began in 1619 when twenty Africans were brought to Jamestown, Virginia, and sold to the colonists. During the early nineteenth century, opposition to slavery increased. Many people felt it was wrong to own another human being and objected to the cruel way the slaves were treated. Support for slavery was strongest in the South, where the large plantations depended on slave labour.

This painting of a slave market looks peaceful and orderly and the slaves are neatly dressed. But if you look closely you can see the suffering associated with slavery. These people are being bought and sold as if they were cattle. The auctioneer is probably telling his listeners that the young woman for sale is a fine specimen, strong and fit and likely to bear healthy children. She is holding the hand of a young man, perhaps her husband. They may be sold as a pair. Or they may be sold to different buyers and never see each other again, as often happened. It was also common for parents to be separated from children.

Generally the slaves bore their suffering patiently, but some ran away. If a runaway slave was caught, he or she would be severely punished, usually by beating. The system depended on fear; if slaves did not fear capture, they would naturally try to run away. In fact, many thousands did manage to escape with the help of the 'Underground Railroad'. This was not a railway but a loose network of people who provided hiding places and guided runaways to freedom in the North and in Canada.

Many slaves even rebelled. In 1831 a Virginia slave named Nat Turner led seventy-five other slaves in a rebellion that killed fifty-seven whites before it was crushed by the state militia. Nearly a hundred slaves, including innocent ones, were killed; Turner was tried and hanged.

This man is examining a woman's teeth, as though she were a horse, to see if she is worth the price being asked. Most slave owners took reasonably good care of their slaves because a sickly slave was of little use to them.

The Slave Market
by Friedrich Schulz (1823–75). This painting is in the Hirshhorn Museum, Washington, DC.

THE CIVIL WAR

The civil war between North and South was caused by two major issues – slavery and states' rights. The southern states, where slavery was legal, wanted to take slavery into the western territories. Northerners wanted to stop the spread of slavery. Southerners also objected to interference by the central government and wanted to be able to reject any federal law they did not like.

In 1860, Abraham Lincoln was elected President. Lincoln was opposed to the spread of slavery, and the South feared he would abolish it altogether. The southern states left the Union, claiming they had a legal right to do so, and called themselves the Confederate States of America.

When the southern states left the Union, they seized all federal property such as forts and government buildings. In December 1869, the commander of a fort at Charleston, South Carolina, refused to surrender. He moved his troops to Fort Sumter on an island in Charleston's harbour, where the Union forces held out against the Confederates. In April 1861, Lincoln sent supply ships to Fort Sumter. Just before the ships arrived, the Confederates fired on the fort and forced a surrender. The American Civil War had begun.

The Civil War was the scene of the first battle ever fought between ironclad ships. At the beginning of the war the North placed a naval blockade around the South to prevent the Confederacy from trading with other nations. The Confederates, who had no navy, got hold of an old Union ship, the *Merrimack*, covered it with iron plates and fitted it with ten guns. An ironclad ship could easily destroy a wooden ship. When the North learned of the *Merrimack's* transformation, they built their own iron ship, the *Monitor*. It carried only two guns, but it had a revolving turret so the guns could fire in any direction. This strange-looking ship was described as 'a cheesebox on a raft'.

On 8 March 1862, the *Merrimack* attacked and sank the 50-gun USS *Cumberland*. That night the *Monitor* arrived on the scene. It met the *Merrimack*, and for four and a half hours the two strange vessels fired round after round at each other. Neither ship won the battle, and the blockade was to remain in effect throughout the war. But naval history had been made. From that moment, wooden warships were out of date. Iron, and then steel, battle-ships would, in future, rule the waves.

Battle of the Ironclads, Monitor v Merrimack
A print published by Currier and Ives in 1862.

Many artists depicted this famous battle between the two ironclads in paintings and engravings.

THE BATTLE OF GETTYSBURG

For the first two years the Civil War went badly for the North. But in the summer of 1863, two Union victories, at Gettysburg and Vicksburg, turned the tide in favour of the Union.

Late in June, the Confederates under General Robert E. Lee advanced into Pennsylvania, intending to capture its capital, Harrisburg. On 1 July they met a troop of Union cavalry just outside the town of Gettysburg. By the following day, 65,000 Confederate and 85,000 Union troops, under General Gordon Meade, had arrived at the spot. The Battle of Gettysburg lasted from 1 to 3 July.

The most important engagement, 'Pickett's Charge', took place on the third day. The Union had borne heavy losses, but they held firm on Cemetery Ridge, and General Lee decided to attack. Led by General George Pickett, three divisions – 15,000 men – marched across open land towards the Union position. With their flags and gleaming bayonets, the Confederate forces looked, said one Union soldier, 'magnificent, grim, irresistible'.

When they were about 630 m away, the Union artillery opened fire. The two outer flanks collapsed, but Pickett's own division kept on coming. They surged up on to the ridge – the moment caught in this painting. The Union troops closed in on them. Of the 15,000 Confederate soldiers, some 6,500 were killed, wounded or captured.

When the battle of Gettysburg was finally over the casualties shocked the nation. More than 28,000 Confederate and 23,000 Union soldiers were killed or wounded. On 4 July, General Lee began his retreat south. He took full blame for the disaster; this was one of the few misjudgements of his career, but it was a fatal one.

Pickett's Charge
by Thure de Thulstrup (1848–1930).
It is in a private collection.

The same day brought news of another Union victory: General Ulysses S. Grant had captured Vicksburg, a Confederate stronghold on the Mississippi River. This opened the river once more to Union ships. It was, as someone said at the time, 'the best Fourth of July since 1776'.

As you can see from this detail, a great many horses as well as humans were killed in the Battle of Gettysburg.

LIBERTY AND A NEW LIFE

On 28 October 1886, the Statue of Liberty was unveiled in New York Harbor. The statue was a gift from the people of France to commemorate the alliance of France and the USA during the War of Independence and as a tribute to the American spirit of liberty.

The thousands of immigrants who came to the USA in hopes of a better life for themselves and their families sailed through New York Harbor. As they passed by the Statue of Liberty, they would be comforted by the words carved on its base from a poem by Emma Lazarus: 'Give me your tired, your poor, your huddled masses yearning to breathe free . . . I lift my lamp beside the Golden Door.'

By the early 1900s, as many as 15,000 immigrants would arrive every day. Most immigrants came from southern Europe, especially the poorer parts of Italy; many Jews came from Russia, where they were cruelly persecuted. Some immigrants came in search of political freedom. The new arrivals tended to live near people from their own country who had already settled in the USA. This way they had neighbours who spoke their language and could help them adjust to American life. Many stayed in New York, giving that city the international flavour it has today.

The newly arrived immigrants often lived in conditions hardly better than those they had left behind. Employers took advantage of this steady supply of cheap labour. Trade unions had only recently been formed, and people worked in factories for low pay and in unpleasant, even dangerous, conditions. Many immigrants lived crammed together in slums. In time, though, most did manage to make a better life. They learned English and became American citizens. Their different cultures and traditions have given the USA a richly varied character.

Unveiling the Statue of Liberty by Edward Moran (1829–1901). This painting is in a private collection.

THE RAILWAY

The railway played a key role in the growth of the USA. It linked existing towns and cities and helped to create new ones. Once the railway had arrived, transporting goods became much faster and cheaper than it had been by horse-drawn vehicles. And people could now travel much more easily than ever before.

At the end of the Civil War in 1865, there were 56,000 km of railway track in the USA. But there was no line connecting the rail systems in the east and west. People had to travel across the plains by horseback, coach or covered wagon. In 1866 two rail companies – the Union Pacific, starting from California, and the Central Pacific, starting from Nebraska – began a race across the mountains and plains towards each other, laying track for a new transcontinental railway. Three years later, on 10 May 1869, they met in Utah, at a place they named Promontory Point. There they joined the two lines of track with a golden spike.

Manchester Valley
by Joseph Pickett (1848–1918).
It is in the Museum of Modern Art, New York.

This painting commemorates the coming of the railway to New Hope, Pennsylvania, in 1891.

Snowbound
An American railway scene by Currier and Ives dated 1871.

With the opening of the transcontinental railway, more and more settlers moved west.

More people than ever settled on the Great Plains. They bought land along the route on credit from the railway. The government parcelled out 'homesteads' to settlers. If they worked the land for five years, it became theirs. Between 1870 and 1890, the population of Kansas and Nebraska increased sixfold. Small towns along the railway lines grew into big cities. Chicago, where trains from east and west met, grew from 444,000 in 1870 to 1,700,000 in 1900.

THE WILD WEST

Life was harsh on the frontier; a person had to be tough to survive. But the West held great promise to those who were looking for opportunities or adventures. At the same time, this untamed part of the country attracted those who wished to be free of the laws of civilization.

Among the glamorous figures of the Old West was the cowboy. He lived close to nature, sleeping under the stars, herding cattle to grazing lands and driving them along trails to the railway stockyards for shipment east. A cowboy's life was also dangerous, with the constant risk of an attack from Native Americans whose lands were being invaded, or a fight with rival herders over a water hole.

One such attack is shown in this painting by Frédéric Remington, who painted many scenes of western life. This painting is typical of Remington's work, which was sympathetic but never sentimental about life in the West. Here in the parched landscape men are prepared to kill or be killed for a source of water.

Fight for the Waterhole
by Frédéric Remington (1861–1909). This painting is in the Museum of Fine Arts, Houston, Texas.

Rustlers at Work
by Harold von Schmidt (1861–1909). This painting is part of a private collection.

Cattle often roamed freely over the vast areas of land that were part of the larger ranches. Cattle thieves, known as rustlers, would rope the cattle and lead them off the ranch to sell to other ranchers. One way to stop rustlers was to brand the cattle with a mark so that a rancher could recognize his own animals.

Violence often erupted in the towns, as everyone who has seen a 'western' knows. Anything would serve to set off a fight between the men who drank and gambled in the saloons. Gangs of outlaws often preyed upon towns and farms. The marshal and his men needed to be as skilled with a gun as these outlaws were in order to enforce the law. One of the most famous American lawmen, 'Wild Bill' Hickok, served as marshal of several Kansas towns and became known as the 'fastest gun in the West'.

In addition to the threat of violence, settlers faced the day-to-day hardships of life in a hostile climate. Winters on the Great Plains are savage, and summers are extremely hot. With no woodland, settlers often had to build their houses from blocks of dried sod, called 'prairie marble'. For fuel they used dried buffalo dung.

The loneliness and bleakness of life on the frontier were more than some people could endure. Some went mad; some gave up and went home. But most stayed put, and gradually they succeeded in taming the 'wild' West.

'THE YANKS ARE COMING'

The First World War broke out in 1914. It was fought between the Central Powers (Germany, Austria-Hungary, Bulgaria and Turkey) and the Allies (France, Russia, Britain and Italy). In 1917, the USA entered the war on the side of the Allies. This marked the beginning of the nation's role as a leading player on the world stage.

When the First World War broke out in 1914, most Americans were determined to stay out of it. Although most people's sympathies lay with the Allies, it was felt that the war was Europe's business. The USA continued to trade with Britain, and in order to break up this trade, Germany made submarine attacks on unarmed merchant ships. Several hundred Americans were killed. It was then discovered that Germany was trying to get Mexico to join in an alliance against the USA. On 6 April 1917, the USA entered the war on the side of the Allies.

The two million American servicemen who went overseas were fit, well-equipped and full of hope. The Europeans were exhausted and crushed after three years of slaughter. Months would pass without either side gaining more than a few metres of ground. The arrival of fresh troops helped the Allies to launch a counter-offensive. In 1918 the Central Powers surrendered, and on 11 November the Armistice was signed.

Out of 65 million troops who fought in the war on both sides, some 10 million were killed and about 20 million wounded. American casualties were relatively light: 53,000 killed and 215,000 wounded. The survivors returned home confident that they had, in President Woodrow Wilson's words, made the world 'safe for democracy'. People called it 'the war to end wars'. The country's economy went from strength to strength. The good times seemed here to stay.

Allies' Day
by Childe Hassam (1859–1935). This painting is in the Hirshhorn Museum, Washington, DC.

This parade down Fifth Avenue in New York City captures the patriotic excitement aroused by the USA's decision to enter the First World War. The flags of the most important Allied countries – Britain and France – are flying alongside the American Stars and Stripes.

THE GREAT DEPRESSION

In October 1929 the good times came abruptly to an end with the crash of the New York Stock Exchange. Share prices fell by 40 per cent within a few weeks, and the country began to slide into the 'Great Depression'. Companies went out of business, and the people left unemployed had no money to buy goods, causing more companies to go out of business. Many banks failed as people rushed to withdraw their savings. Those who arrived too late lost their money. Once-prosperous businesspeople were reduced to begging in the streets.

Almost a quarter of the nation's wage earners were out of work during the Depression, and even those who had jobs were faced with hard times. Farmers were among the hardest-hit. They had not shared in the prosperity of the 1920s. Crop prices were already low when the Depression began, and they dropped much further as demand fell. The suffering of mid-western farmers was increased in the mid-1930s by terrible dust storms. A period of drought had left the topsoil dry and powdery. When high winds swept over the Great Plains, hundreds of millions of tonnes of topsoil were blown away. Farmers and their families fled the 'Dust Bowl', as the area became known, and went in search of jobs as migrant workers. This famous photograph on page 40 shows a Texan family leaving their farm, which has been destroyed by dust storms.

◀ ***Farmer Leaving the Land*** by the American photographer Dorothea Lange (1895–1965).

Dorothea Lange is best known for her photographs of farmers and migrant workers in the Depression years.

When Franklin D. Roosevelt was elected President in 1932, he promised to take action to end the Depression. 'The only thing we have to fear is fear itself,' he said as he took office. His first step was to pass special laws to prevent more banks from collapsing. He then introduced a programme of measures, known as the 'New Deal', that were designed to help those in need and bring about an economic recovery. A federal government agency was set up to provide the individual states with money to feed the hungry. Laws were passed to help farmers and home-owners who were in danger of losing their property because they could not keep up with their mortgage payments. The unemployed were given such jobs as road-building. Among the many reforms Roosevelt introduced was the Social Security Act, which provided unemployment benefit and pensions for the elderly.

Although the New Deal went a long way in helping people and getting the nation back to work, a complete economic recovery was a long and slow process. The effects of the Depression lasted until 1939, when the Second World War broke out in Europe.

'THE MARINES HAVE LANDED'

On 1 September 1939, German troops marched into Poland. Two days later Britain and France declared war on Germany, and the Second World War had begun. It was to last until 1945 and involve all the great powers of the world and most of the smaller nations. At first the USA was determined to stay out of what was seen as a European war. Then, on 7 December 1941, Japan attacked the American naval base at Pearl Harbor, Hawaii, killing 2,400 soldiers and sailors and destroying many ships and planes. The following day the USA declared war on Japan and joined Britain and the other Allied countries in the war against the Axis powers – Germany, Italy and Japan.

▲ At first glance it looks as though the Marines are having to struggle hard to raise the flag. Or it may be that all these hands reflect the men's eagerness to take part in a great historic event. What do you think?

American troops were soon fighting in Europe, North Africa and the Pacific. The Battle of Midway, in June 1942, marked the turning point of the Pacific war, as the USA repulsed a Japanese attack on this American-held island. Slowly, the Americans went on to capture vital positions in the vast Pacific.

In the last months of the war, in February and March 1945, the two sides fought one of the war's fiercest battles on Iwo Jima, a Japanese island about 1,200 km south of Tokyo. Iwo Jima held a Japanese air base that the Americans planned to use for launching an attack on Japan itself.

The Marines landed on the island on 19 February. Four days later they captured Mount Suribachi, and here they raised the American flag. The event was captured in a famous war photograph, which was later translated into a bronze sculpture. This statue stands near Arlington Cemetery, a reminder of the heroism of American servicemen in the Second World War.

After another three weeks of fighting, Iwo Jima was finally captured, at a cost of 6,855 American lives. In the end, an invasion of Japan was ruled out. A new, more efficient way

United States Marine Corps War Memorial
This sculpture by Felix de Weldon is based on a photograph by Joe Rosenthal. It is located in Arlington, Virgina

The U.S. Marines are raising the flag on Mount Suribachi on the Japanese island of Iwo Jima.

of getting Japan to surrender had been developed: the atomic bomb. After bombs were dropped on Hiroshima (6 August) and Nagasaki (9 August), Japan surrendered. Iwo Jima now belongs once more to Japan.

A WORLD POWER

The USA emerged from the Second World War as the most powerful country on earth and soon began to take a more active role in world affairs.

The most important feature of the post-war years was the Cold War. This refers to the hostility between the USA and its European allies, on one side, and the USSR and its allies, on the other. At the root of the Cold War was conflict between the political and economic system in the West – democracy and capitalism – and that in the East – Communism. The USA's campaign against the spread of Communism led to its involvement in the affairs of many other countries and to two wars – the Korean War (1950–53) and the Vietnam War (1964–73). The Cold War, came to an end with the break-up of the USSR in 1992.

The 1960s were marked by protests – from Blacks who were frustrated by their unfair treatment at the hands of Whites, by women who wanted the same opportunities as men, and by young people who were dissatisfied with the way that the older generation was running the country. These protests did eventually bring about changes of attitude, but not before two heroes of the 1960s were assassinated - President John F. Kennedy in 1963, and the civil rights leader Martin Luther King in 1968. The 1960s also saw the beginning of the space programme. In 1969, the Apollo 11 mission landed the first man on the moon. The USA still leads the world in space exploration.

Today, the USA, like most industrialized countries, is faced with many problems, such as environmental pollution, economic slowdown and the growing cost of providing social services. But the country that was founded on the principles of equality and freedom will surely be able to find ways to assure a prosperous and peaceful future.

Signs
A screen print by Robert Rauschenberg (b.1925). The print is held in the Cleveland Museum of Art.

This collage shows some of the major figures and events in the recent history of the USA: the Vietnam War, the space programme, President John F. Kennedy, who was assassinated in 1963, the pop singer Janis Joplin, and Martin Luther King and Senator Robert Kennedy, who were both assassinated in 1968.

CONVOY FOLLOWING

GLOSSARY

Alliance A group of countries agreeing to act together.

Ambassador Someone who is sent to a foreign country to represent his or her own country.

Armistice A temporary stopping of war by mutual agreement, before signing a peace treaty.

Blockade A cutting off of a port or region by an enemy so that supplies and equipment cannot get in or out.

Capitalism An economic system whereby goods are produced by privately owned companies.

Capitol The building in which the US Congress meets in Washington, DC.

Cavalry Troops mounted on horses.

Civil war A war between citizens of one country.

Collage A picture made by pasting paper and other materials on to a flat surface.

Colony A region ruled by people from another country. Settlers in a colony are called colonists.

Communism A system of government under which all industry and commerce is owned by the state and there is no private property.

Delegates People elected to represent others at a meeting.

Expedition A journey for a special purpose, such as exploring and mapping new territory.

First World War The war (1914–18) fought by the Central Powers – Germany, Austria-Hungary, Turkey and Bulgaria – against the Allies – France, Russia, Britain, Italy and the USA.

Immigrant Someone who comes to another country to settle there.

Independence Being a totally separate, self-governing country.

Marshal An officer appointed by the federal government to a region to carry out court rules, enforce the laws and keep the peace.

Mennonites Members of a Christian church founded in the sixteenth century in Germany. They believe in simple living and plain dress.

Migrant workers Farm workers who move from place to place to harvest seasonal crops.

Militia An army made up of citizens who are called out in a time of emergency.

TIMELINE

- **1492** Columbus lands in the Caribbean
- **1587** Colony founded at Roanoke island
- **1607** Jamestown, Virginia founded
- **1619** Slaves first brought to Virginia
- **1620** Pilgrims in *Mayflower* land in Massachusetts
- **1681** William Penn founds Pennsylvania
- **1773** Boston Tea Party
- **1774** Meeting of the First Continental Congress
- **1775** Beginning of the War of Independence
- **1776** Battle of Trenton
- Declaration of Independence (4 July)
- **1778** France signs treaty with the Americans
- **1781** Battle of Yorktown
- **1791** Treaty with the Cherokee nation
- **1803** President Jefferson buys Louisiana Territory from France
- **1804** Lewis and Clark travel to the west coast
- **1812–14** War with Britain
- **1828** US army moves the Cherokees off their land
- **1848** Gold found near Sacramento, California
- **1849** Gold rush in California
- **1860** President Lincoln elected
- **1861** Civil War between Confederates and Unionists
- **1862** Battle of the ironclads
- **1863** Battle of Gettysburg
- **1865** Civil War ends
- **1886** Statue of Liberty unveiled

Mortgage To pledge your house or property as security to someone who lends you money.
Patriotic To be inspired by love of one's country.
Petition A special request to an authority.
Pilgrims People who travel to a holy place. The Plymouth colonists were called Pilgrims because they travelled to avoid religious injustice.
Quakers . Members of the Society of Friends, a Christian religious sect founded in England in the 1600s. Quakers reject violence and war.
Saloon A place where alcoholic drinks are sold to drink on the premises.
Second World War The war (1939–45) fought by Germany, Italy and Japan (Axis Powers) against Britain, USSR, France, USA and their allies.
Sect A branch of a larger religious group.
Stocks and shares Portions of capital i.e. money or other assets of a business held by investors.
Slavery The custom of buying and selling slaves, who are people owned as the property of others.
USSR Union of Soviet Socialist Republics. The USSR was made up of 15 republics, which in 1992 split up into independent countries. The largest country of the former USSR is Russia.

BOOKS TO READ

American Frontier by Nigel Smith (Wayland, 1991)
The United States by Ian James (Watts, 1990)
The United States by Susan Williams (Wayland, 1990)
The United States of America by Daphne Butler (Simon and Schuster, Young Books, 1991)
The USA since 1945 by Nigel Smith (Wayland, 1989)
Western Art 1600-1800 by Christopher McHugh (Wayland, 1994)

For older readers:

United States History in Notable Works of Art by Edith Pavese (Abrams, 1993)

1869	Union Pacific and Central Pacific railtracks meet in Utah
1914	Outbreak of First World War
1917	USA enters the war
1918	Armistice signed
1929	New York Stock Excange crash
1932	Franklin D. Roosevelt becomes President
1930s	Great Depression
1939	Outbreak of Second World War
1941	Japan attacks Pearl Harbor (7 December) USA declares war on Japan (8 December)
1942	Battle of Midway
1944	US and allied landings in Normandy
1945	(February and March) Battle of Iwo Jima (August) Atomic bombs dropped on Hiroshima and Nagasaki Surrender of Japan - Second World War ends Cold War begins
1950-53	Korean War
1963	Civil rights campaign in Alabama led by Martin Luther King President J.F. Kennedy presents Civil Rights Bill to Congress (November) Kennedy assassianted
1964–73	Vietnam War
1968	Assassination of Martin Luther King
1969	First moon landing
1992	End of the Cold War.

INDEX

The entries in **bold** refer to the illustrations

Adams, John 15, **15**
Allies' Day 38, **39**
American flag 17, **17**, **39**
Apollo space programme 44

Battle of the Ironclads: Monitor vs. Merrimack **29**
Bierstadt, Albert 20
Boone, Daniel 20
Boston 12
Boston Tea Party 12
Boston Tea Party **12**
Boughton, George Henry 7
Britain 6, 10, 12, 16, 18 , 38, 42

California 8, 9, 24, 34
California gold rush 24–5
Canada 8, 18, 20, 26
Cherokees 22, **23**
Chicago 35
Civil War 28–31, 34
Clark, William 21, **21**
Cold War 44
Colonies 6, 8, 9
colonists 4, 6, 12, 26
Columbus, Christopher 4
Concord, Battle of 13
Confederacy 28, 30
Congress 14, 15, 16
Currier and Ives 12, 29, 35

Declaration of Independence 14–15, 20
Declaration of Independence **14-15**
Delaware 8
Depression, the Great 40–41

Farmer Leaving the Land 40, **41**
federal government 18, 22 , 28
Fight for the Waterhole 36
First World War 38
forty-niners 24
Fourth of July, Center Square, Philidelphia **19**
France 16, 20, 21, 32. 38
Franklin, Benjamin 10, 15, **15**

Georgia 22
Gettysburg 30
Gettysburg, battle of 30, **31**
Grant, Ulysses S. 31
Great Plains 35, 37, 41

Hassam, Childe 38
Hancock, John 15, **15**
Harrisburg 30
Hickok, Wild Bill 37
Hicks, Edward 10, 11
homesteads 35

immigrants 32
Intolerable Acts 12, 14
Iwo Jima 42, 43, **43**

Jackson, Andrew 22
Jamestown 6, 26
Jefferson, Thomas 14, **15**, 20

Kennedy, John F. 44, **45**
Kennedy, Robert 44, 45
Kentucky 20
King, Jr. Martin Luther 44, **45**
Korean War 44
Krimmel, John L 19

Lange, Dorothea 41
Lee, Robert E. 30
Leutze, Emanuel G. 17
Lexington, Battle of 13
Lewis, Meriwether 21, **21**
Lincoln, Abraham 6, 28
Lindneaux, Robert 22
Louisiana 8, 20, 21

Manchester Valley **34**
Manner of Their Fishing, The **4**, **5**
Marshall, James 24
Massachusetts 6, 12
Mayflower 6
Mayflower Compact 6
Meade, Gordon 30
Mennonites 9
Mexican War 24
Midnight Ride of Paul Revere 13
minutemen 12
Monroe, James 18
Moran, Edward ii, 32
Mount, William 25

'naive' artists 10
Native Americans 4, **5**, 6, 9, **9**, 10, 20, 22–3, **23**, 36
Nebraska 34, 35
New Deal 41
New Jersey 16
New Mexico 8
New Orleans 21
New York 8, 16
North Carolina 4, 22
Northwest Territory 20

Oklahoma 22
On the Oregon Trail **20**
Oregon 18, 21

Penn, William **8**, 9
Penn's Treaty with the Indians **8**, **9**
Pennsylvania 8, 9, 10, 30, 34
Philadelphia 9, 14, 16, 18, **19**
Pickett, George 30
Pickett's Charge **31**
Pilgrims 6, **7**
Pilgrims Going to Church **6-7**
pioneers 20, 21, **21**
plantations 10, 26
Plymouth Colony 6

Polk, James 24

Quakers 9, 10

railways 24, 34–5, **34**, **35**, 36
Rauschenberg, Robert 44
Reading News of the Gold Rush **24**, **25**
Remmington, Frederic 36
Residence of David Twining, The **10**, **11**
Revere, Paul 12**, 13**
Rosenthal, Joe 43
Roosevelt, Franklin D. 41
Russell, Alfred 21
Rustlers at Work 37

St Louis 21
Sacagawea 21, **21**
Sacagawea Guides Lewis and Clark **21**
San Francisco 24
Santa Clara de Asis 9, **9**
Santa Clara de Asis **9**
Second World War 41, 42–3
Schmidt, Harold von 37
Schutz, Friedrich 27
settlers 9, 10, 20, 35, 37
Signs 44, **45**
Slave Market, The **26-7**
slaves 10, 26, **27**
Snowbound 35
Spain 4, 8, 9, 20
Statue of Liberty **ii**, 32, **33**
Sutter, John 24

Tennessee 22
Texas 8
Thanksgiving 6
Thirteen Colonies 6, 12, 14, 17
Thulstrup, Thure de 31
Trail of Tears, The 22, **23**
Trenton, Battle of 16
Turner, Nat 26

United States Marine Corps War Memorial **42**, **43**
Unveiling the Statue of Liberty 32, **33**

Vicksburg, Battle of 30, 31
Vietnam War 44
Virginia 16, 26

War of 1812 18
War of Independence 12, 13, 15, 22, 32
Washington, D.C. 18
Washington, George 14, 16, 17, **17**
Washington Crossing the Delaware **16-17**
Weldon, Felix 43
West, Benjamin 9
White, John 4
Wilson, Woodrow 38
Wood, Grant 13

Yorktown, Battle of 16